D1824091

Find My Happy

DANDYLANDY

STORIES FOR YOUR SOUL

www.dandylandybooks.com

ISBN: 978-1-7391917-0-2
Copyright © 2022 Rebecca Dandy
Illustrations and design made by Ira Baykovska

This book is dedicated to all of the little people, especially my little people, Skye, Riley & Oliver.

I hope you always find your happy :)

Little Luka Logan, woke up feeling snappy, he looked around his playhouse thinking, "I must have lost my happy".

Not sure where he had left it, he took off in a craze,

he wondered where it could have gone,
as he hadn't felt good for days.

He visited his toy room and looked
underneath his teddy,
he climbed up on his treehouse
ladder, holding himself steady.

He looked through all the windows
and walked around the garden,
when he heard a massive, "OUCH,
why, young man, I beg your pardon!"...

Little Luka Logan, jumped back and gasped in fright,
he had trodden on a monkey, now standing in plain sight!

Mr Monkey yelped, "What on earth are you trying to do?"
"Please remove my luscious tail from underneath your shoe".

Luka looked apologetically at Mr Monkey's glare,
in a timid voice he uttered,
"I'm so sorry for not seeing you there".

"Well now, not to worry, you just gave me a little fright".
"You look most upset Luka, are you feeling quite alright?"

Luka felt deflated and turned his gaze away,
"I cannot find my happy and so I'm feeling sad today".

"Now Luka my dear boy,
let's take a moment to stop your fear".
"Your happiness may wander off
but it is always somewhere near".
"You see it's very normal for you to feel this way".

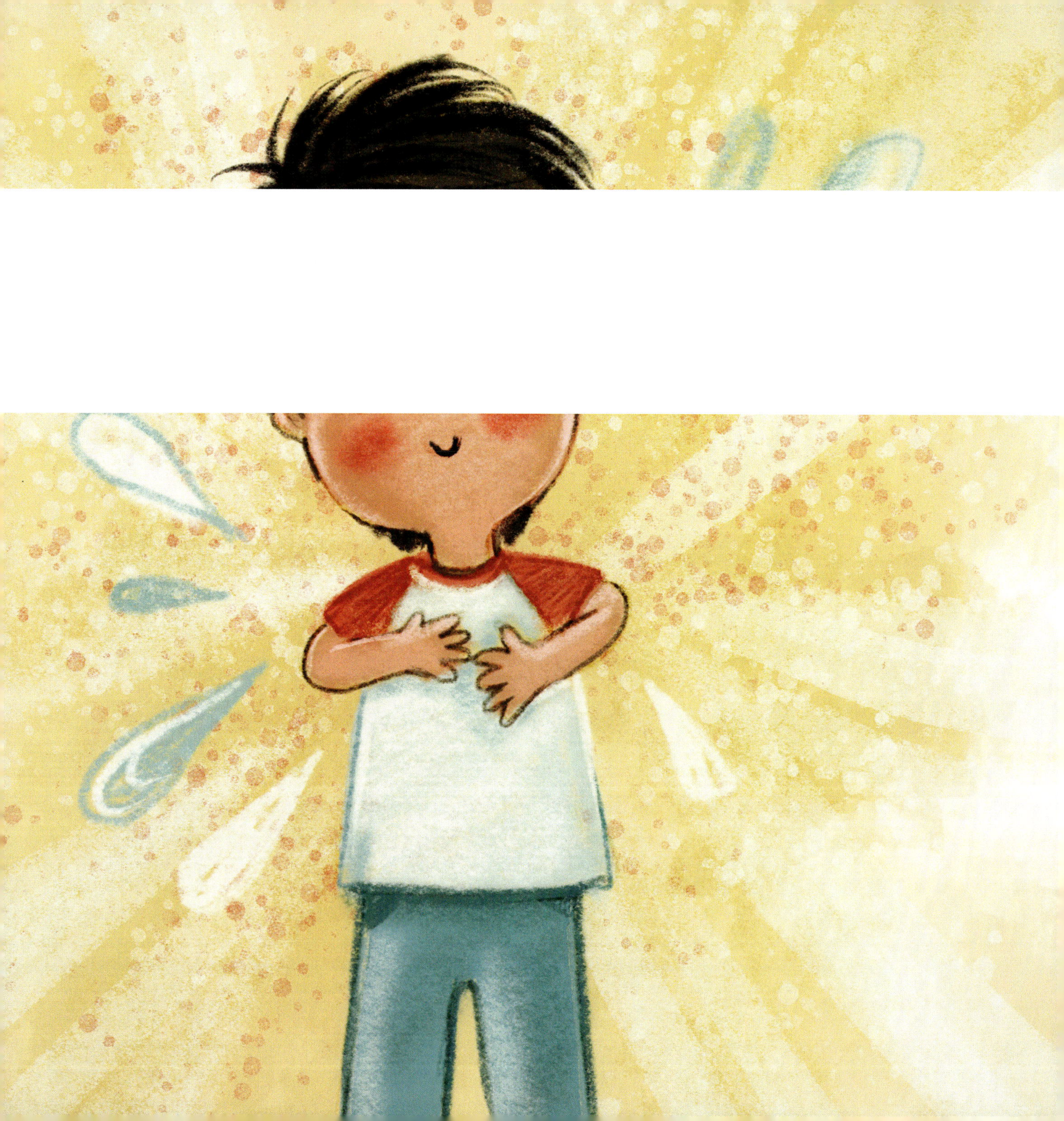

"Sometimes we're very happy and happy is where we stay".
"Other times we may begin, to slip, slide and fall".
"It is in these testing times, we learn to rise above it all".
"Look within Luka, for happiness is a part of you".

"It cannot be found in a toy or a thing
and it won't be hiding in a shoe".
"Happiness is not a place or a person,
it's a state of being, of that, I'm certain".

"Please do not worry,
or try to force it in a hurry.
You simply need to sit with this
sadness in your tummy".
"Whenever I feel sad,
I remember what I love,
like a beautiful walk in nature
or a warm and friendly hug".

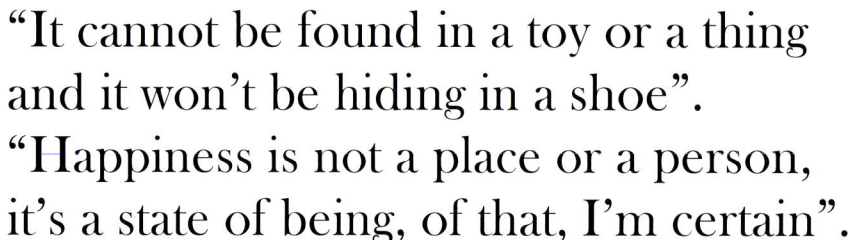

"Oh, thank you Mr Monkey, your words have helped a lot. I feel much better knowing that I haven't lost the plot".

Luka began to smile as he felt comfort from within.
His smile was so contagious, even Mr Monkey began to grin!

"I hope other boys and girls know it's okay to feel snappy,
my biggest wish for the world is that
everyone finds their happy".